A NEO TR

JAMIE STEWART,

A
Neo
Tropical
Companion.

:

cover design by joe stewart

printed by lightning source, milton keynes
in an endless edition (version 120126)
ISBN 978-90-817091-4-9

uitgeverij, den haag
shtëpia botuese, tiranë
publishing house, durham

www.uitgeverij.cc

for Joseph Stewart & Cory McCulloch

dedicating this
to a woman she had wronged
it burst into flame

*

if your body stinks
you could live in a mud hut
and seal up the door

*

in the eye of God
certainty of love and rest
how to let it in?

a bruted short man
jockey behind a horse cart
you beat my uncle

*

man, i want to die
i have such a fucking head ache
and i am bummed out

*

hello nephew Ace!
your red hair is three years old
i miss you and Joe

my hair looks so bad
samurai chop it all down
my head can go too

＊

Ace, my grandfather
a closeted ship's captain
vodka and a wife

＊

i feel ill at ease
the solution is vodka
stave off knowing why

thinking at the gym
there is no one cute at all
that's why we are here

*

incessant chirping
the trees are filled with those frogs
their blood on crows beaks

*

a cramp in your guts
brings to mind a sharpened spoon
cut as a grapefruit

my cat has gained weight
merely awaiting a crow
he won't chase his toys

*

you are cute at night
little and cut mouth open
stoned out of your mind

*

untie the white thread
insecure the casing guts
chorizo blood rains

when i fail myself
the devil bites my eye ball
and i see a cow

*

hallucination
fantastical hummingbirds
drenched in humid sweat

*

smog of Great Ani
damn the devil's bird screeches
cringe out all our dusks

dear God pity us
for now, do not turn away
from your begging horde

*

when all else fails you
beg them to pay attention
that's why they like dogs

*

revealing distrust
heated and sweaty arm pits
"i believe in you"

your cock is sugar
granulate it up my ass
my tears are candy

*

band mates fall like weeds
in an orgy of revenge
directed at pop

*

caffeine and sugar
drive my mind to admit ruin
more candy, more pop

war shot off your legs
you fucked your boss and a dwarf
his cock was immense

   *

face like a danish
packed with spoiled goose fatty jam
no longer my boss

   *

i hear my father
his howling in the shower
reverberations

please don't talk to me
there is something to think of…
weevils in caramel

*

sweet Ku Klux Klan
white chocolate in your shape
poke into my tits

*

cameo pistol
could bring us to be true friends
think of me this way

Turin, Italy
chocolate and truest friends
smash it and kiss it

*

late at night i think
i want to buy a pistol
chromed in gleaming black

*

a pile of hacked feet
poked by savage white killers
the butcher's display

wake up! be aware!
your heros would pat your head
white emulation

*

white board Bible verse
of vengeance and White hatred
gas station display

*

eating like a pig
the executioner's hood
could be an option

American flag
stitched onto a lost man's coat
eyes glazed by strip clubs

*

air strip awaiting
chance grants the capuchin bird
and what else but tears

*

his hero in shame
it haunted him constantly
his father's weeping

i miss my mother
bad things have happened to her
she lives in the woods

*

soured afternoon
white might infected play yard
'04 Moscow

*

no weeds in our yard
they cleared out the vacant lot
cardinals are gone too

vasectomising
freaked by the baby shower
you weep in the car

*

the stray cat dead stares
in my house cats racing eyes
Bark! they hear a dog

*

soda makes you fat
so does sitting on your ass
and rating people

acne on your lip
dog filled BMW
what is wrong with you?

*

dig into the earth
a mandrake makes you pregnant
like lice from Hades

*

green tea has returned
respite from new sadder days
they came suddenly

stunned into sad awe
in flight over Greenland's sheets
what remains of Earth

*

crush us slave digger
resentment of your defeats
bursts in arrogance

*

sudden blackness
so when you ask what is wrong
you know it is you

"out from the darkness
the cat considers our lamp
returns to darkness"

*

the lamp is broken
set next to the loveless bed
glass is everywhere

*

a mother would share
her sex life with her first son
hate and more than hate

one or another
considering resentments
against happiness

*

to pee in the bed
is it one that you can't share?
sadistic Chicago

*

faded party mom
blonde dyed hair, leopard skin purse
listens to her son

it is hard to find
isolated cement slabs
to burn a book on

*

my butthole hurting
my rash will not go away
disflattered in age

*

cling to your creme pies
running across the freeway
do not drop those pies!

allow me to push
a white pastille in your butt
poo it in my hand

*

at nine years of age
you seem like a cleaned fossil
of the first genius

*

book of nude photos
husband and wife with strangers
question your true birth

little girls and boys
your bones poking through your skin
imagination

*

a secret gay life
bonded in molestations
upon your daughter

*

it has been a while
since i was certain of this
and yet still so lost

half asleep, half dull
in self-consideration
please fucking kill me

*

AIDS destroyed your bones
a split invades childhood years
you'll have no others

*

get out of my way!
anxious gorgon of morning
too frightened to work

jerk off on the floor
look down and take off your shoes
clean it with your socks

*

sweet expensive scotch
you were once so dear to me
my money is gone

*

can i thank you with
overly expensive shoes
Isle of Approval

surrounded by work
dry cleaning fed all of you
yet you still love clothes

*

the money is gone
replaced by crushed, iron stress
i will suck your dick

*

my throat feels so tight
like it could break off a dick
has a bee stung me?

when your back is turned
a knife's whistle passed your ear
throat cutting gestures

*

my cat eats bird seed
i hear a bomb exploding
now it is flying

*

it was your birthday
now AIDS just sleeps inside you
congratulations

Anarchists hand bomb
blows the Absurdist's pants off
they they fuck in blood

*

pumpkin headed man
don't choke on that rubber toy
out of your mouth cat!

*

the bush tit tweets out
"Henry Cowell loves you Karl!"
and your rubber truth

is your kindness truth?
do you intend to use me?
as i will use you

*

pour lighter fluid
on Durham Bull's eyes and smile
blaze filthy symbol

*

banging on white sheet
blood is pouring out your cunt
mixed with cum and lube

your cunt smells deadly
if you piss into a jar
i will drink it all

*

John, with horse's teeth
the funeral's grand entrance
embarrass the dead

*

blood in the toilet
is that from my ass or mouth?
my body is fulfilled

hey, get on your knees!
and put your face to the floor
finish that puzzle!

*

the floor is filthy
one could always but do more
sweeping once a week

*

please just let me watch
i do not want to be touched
dark, imploded lust

it's already dark
we have so much work to do
but then, a hushed fuck

*

could hard drugs help you
to finish a day of work
dressed as Frankenstein?

*

please don't shoot those ducks
aren't they too beautiful?
beyond sportsman's lust

stitched in red vinyl
a mask that leads you to fight
against your dumb face

*

he is so proud of
indiscretions against her
she is beautiful

*

fight over the broom
the garbage bag and the pick
how strange those kids are

the first job you have
will be at a taco truck
or a taco bell

*

gongs and bells clang clang
vibrations flick every heart
ringing tortured bronze

*

the squirrels run away
when the garbage truck rolls by
take it over squirrels!

gag on rotten meat
your boyfriend is turning blue
bluer than the sky

*

screaming at the beach,
"isn't my body enough
to fuck properly?!"

*

the air is butter
Amazonian night sky
my skin is amazed

you want to be kind
in having fucked your own corpse
it's embarrassing

*

people are a drag
you seem to understand this
i am sorry too

*

1970
to fuck and love every man
before the specter

holding out your thumb
run across the valley street
sell your holes at dawn

*

thank you for trying
a promise of forever
you know i'm a sap

*

prom in the valley
how awesome not to have gone!
how totally rad!

your skin is besot
from stress, less sex, from life
love makes me nervous

*

looking down the street
the summer is like a mud
that you want to dry

*

over Kenyan cliffs
forever of flamingos
just missed machetes

cruelly waxed pussy
sore, unfuckable and bald
oh, you missed a spot

*

red bloom at the stem
grafted wax to black currants
graphed by the screen door

*

Krakow balcony
red line slashed star of David
i eat a lemon

pre-teen abortion
that is how funny you are
so break up with me

*

eat bitter melon
then a lemon is paradise
even eat the seeds

*

it's quiet in here
nothing's crashing or breaking
the cats are asleep

"kill them, kill them all!"
soldiers scream at the village
suicidal guilt

*

teenaged obsessions
sex, fame, drugs, guns, knives, his, hers
muthafuckin boss

*

one gang wears purple
the other one wears yellow
run out of colors?

taking advantage
of the guilt of past neglects
to show disrespect

*

malarial girl,
thick yellow sweat on her cot,
thinks her village sucks

*

inject me with drugs
he would hit and beat me down
then i was sold on

three nuns making out
snorting coke in garter belts
high school was stupid

*

my father is dead
my mom works at the graveyard
farting by the urns

*

starling on dead corn
luminescent parasite
destroy your own kind

the catholic school
was destroyed by an earthquake
ha ha you assholes

*

he exposed himself
to you as a little girl
now you are a mom

*

egomaniac
goat riding a human boy
you disappoint me

beep beep beep boop beep
a German synthesizer
leg irons removed

*

my legs are nasty
white blotches of ingrown hair
scrape and amputate

*

holding it inside
stress, frustration, angry sparks
dark in murked restraint

how did you beat AIDS?
like a viking in lava
smiter of gay death!

✳

rice, tofu, kimchi
remove sleet of effort's strain
AH! who else but food?

✳

the floor is moldy
your house keeping is awful
i'm not your father

the white cat whispers
sad stories to the black one
"the cat box is full."

*

the weight is removed
i cannot have a baby
one less life to wreck

*

plantain or yuca
Indian or African
Chinese or whitey

your hair looks perfect
if it's kept under a bush
like a flightless bird

*

on fungused pathway
box turtle eat a mushroom
it stares into space

*

wondrous peckèd head
Pileated woodpecker
look look there it goes!

a vicious white nurse
clenches her thighs and slit shrieks,
"i own your breathing!"

*

bad skin on my thighs
feelings of incompetence
judge of awfulness

*

the flag of Japan
plum in a bowl of white rice
set murderous plum

bald, short sentences
accessible to the poor
like rickets and gout

*

wood blocks and cymbals
bass clarinet and tuba
arise bald faced wrath!

*

pink troll, yellow troll
farm gnome, wood gnome, forest gnome
little human boy

white cat won't come out
her head against the door jam
it could get crushed there

*

stomach is twisting
displeasure of bananas
deforestation

*

stupid yuppie fucks
destroying all this is good
with not much to start

hi naked Eric
that couch looks smooth on your ass
not unlike your chest

*

your eyes are flat dots
imagine you have 12 pairs
all over your head

*

flat face like a pond
that the moon reflects upon
so i make you cry

suffocating towne
suffocating lover's love
gray blocks on my chest

*

astride the red deer
minds functioning unalike
ducking low branches

*

blast through the road block
duck fate of bow and arrow
survive by whiteness

grayed Santa Muerte
conferring with Mal Verde
Mictecacihuatl

*

Capped Heron is perched
on a branch by the river
did you see me too?

*

they see the bird too
unemployed, drunk and older
titmouse on its branch

robins and starlings
black shapes really, not true birds
their songs are less black

*

your pills make you weird
a voice vague as cotton balls
are you happier?

*

tie smurfs to a pole
dipped in childhood's gasoline
melt flickered blue pains

infantilized bully
trampled by a breast-like car
paralyzed cruelty

*

2 years of working
songs about these, the worst thoughts
you are a bummer

*

today was so weird
like a pancake draped on us
spongey and too thick

it's so hot outside
i can only walk around
i'm too drunk to run

*

a million pill bugs
curled into a million balls
roll off a slit throat

*

oh, every horror
that has made you who you are
Northridge, Encino

from behind, i want
to razor slit both your ears
your efforts are bland fizz

*

in how much horror
do you run down the staircase
trampled by the Kims?

*

submitting to claws
the fur is ripped from your throat
unadoptable

Margery, Terry,
John, Liz, Michael, and Florence,
what is heaven like?

*

black fur on red leaves
an indoor cat in heaven
briefly in the yard

*

a contract killer
called my sister for advice
but she was too busy

your parents are dead
there is so much traffic here
your sister is dead

*

given sound advice
don't remember anything
wars come and wars go

*

harvesting the poor
to murder desert children
Fucked East Michigan

twenty years of war
Mogadishu's little girls
staring at the sky

*

this is exciting
watermelons on the track
a train is coming

*

too cold to explore
this desolate wastrel towne
more bullshit to come

one blessèd red sky
looms as the towne's one feature
to suppress such loss

*

it is cold today
yet my underarms are wet
anxious of the snow

*

sit down on the tracks
think of loving your nephew
the wet rail vibrates

ride on your scooter
kissing the back of your shirt
Hanoi in darkness

*

under a light rain
but for dirt, it's edible
dropped watermelon

*

i turn out the light
and shit in total darkness
in gas station booths

hog tied without shame
abyssal stare beyond light
cumming like crazy

*

i hear "can't sleep" grunt
from under the red duvet
it is 4 AM

*

i just dropped my glass
now bourbon is everywhere
mop it with my shirt

i've one fantasy
it has made me cum for years
shameful and common

*

10,000 snow geese
huddling around the light house
what are they eating?

*

would it bother me
to die twelve minutes from now
five would be better

your cock is so big
it curves like the horizon
two balls like two suns

*

nite time fitness elf
metamorphosizing grunts
a curve to a line

*

shutting off the light
ashamed by what i will write
on one could like it

at this age you should
wipe your butt more thoroughly
it's too late to ask

*

there is a scratching…
my hat has flown off my head
a bat's secret home

*

staying out too late
this sun is already down
but i am just up

my balls need a scratch
so do my scalp, eyes and butt
should i use a stick?

*

fly in the ashtray
flake industrial dying
wings flit puffs of shame

*

and if i live twice
i will love you both my lives
yet we have just one

hi Morton Feldman
the jungle surrounds your chimes
endless perfect sound

*

what does he see here
that we could no ever see?
tail flits, ears turning

*

uncomplicated
sprouted from an angry place
Lo! the dull repent

a tick on my balls!
throw the sheets off the damn bed
scream down at my balls

*

the jungle grows dark
black tailed trogon is quiet
a will o wisps glow

*

sickened dull thudding
blotting out violent sound
a ukulele

raped in the shower
by a goblin football coach
being 10 is shit

*

the edge of the bed
classic place to avoid you
slide off spoiled rafts

*

give me back my dreams!
the cat asleep on my head
heisting secret thoughts

staying at my house
your friend that i want to bang
how will i feign sleep?

*

there will be 2 cats
yes, of course they are both black
as likely futures

*

black lip stick on boys
tear open the envelope
a secret goth kiss

your basement technique
kiss tears of cum down my cheek
then swallow my pride

*

so anxious today
there is something sewer-like
what was confidence

*

suicidal thoughts
revive me to breathe deeply
i can leave today

cruised while bird watching
50 vultures in a tree
nervous, i ran off

*

less so than a bird's
my life depends on your grace
red and anxious throat

*

a sewer pipe broke
the basement filled with feces
The Brute breathed deeply

our rock pins the snake
thrashing with scaled colors flared
it wins, we shriek YAAAAAAAAA!

*

hurtle the lobster
over the cliff to the rocks
forever empty

*

on tropic sand bar
note black and turkey vultures
bald heads bowed in shame

your mom's teeth are fucked
eating with your fat brother
denudes an evil

*

a shriek from outside
my brother is on the phone
that means someone died

*

his hood has fallen
and embarrassed olde Grim Death
bald, with missing teeth

my feelings are hurt
congratulations you guys
phony faggots win

*

this towne is empty
brick buildings but not people
thank God, i hate them

*

trying to help me
understand why people love
it hurts my shoulders

bus stop sex worker
bored and waving to no one
her ass is tearing

*

the facts, just the facts
humiliate our effort
to make something good

*

tonite, if you're bored
burn the books you don't want
then take a hot bath

Oh! what is the sound?
a leaf landed in my book
now on my hair too

＊

if the sun kills you
your acorn will grow and live
and save your sister

＊

three boxed porn movies
autographed on the windshield
nicely done hot buck

porn of two sisters
disturbingly similar
could this be this real?

*

it has been ten years
the cloak falls heavier now
since you killed yourself

*

gosh, is that the wind
it sounds bus-accident-esque
it's an accident

i have to go piss
God should have made me a girl
clenching my pussy

*

spindle of thorn vine
have grown a foot since last night
scratch through the window

*

the world eludes them
paws pushing aside the blinds
cats share window space

you are so wasted
your massive juggs glowing red
push them up and piss

*

unsheathed scimitar
shines of decapitations
thrown unto the mob

*

artillery wasps
poo pooed out in racial haste
dark girls will rise up!

you are a dark pest
fuck you all and fuck your war
don't ever return!

*

is it depressing?
a peep show in Budapest
should life omit doom?

*

i asked for God's help
in not drinking for 2 days
but He will not mind

she's tied to a tree
watching her mother pissing
cows drink the yellow

*

no one talks to me
it's so depressing it's true
days and days go by

*

closeted sailor
my grandmother always knew
yet they stayed married

my mother raped me
it was with a popsicle
i had been sleeping

*

a dirty orange
set on his ripped open crotch
it's rotten as well

*

oh hello old chum
it's nice to see you again
eating falafels

pulled off the toilet
your brother, beaten again
hide in the basement

*

celebrate new cat
you have shit in my closet
welcome to your home

*

when we were 19
having fun seemed too easy
throw bikes off a cliff

i won't be home soon
it would be nice to return
you are so horny

*

i miss you crazy
don't forgive all the bruises
as they are my fault

*

Hail! ancient scrub jay
dinosaur like seed eater
sound rips for your call

the trail is obscured
while it was faultless today
poison ivy looms

*

scrub scrub scrub the floor
in chaps made of beige sponges
my thighs are so bruised

*

grasp single focus
a fetish conquered my touch
i want just one thing

UGH! my stomach hurts
it is filling with babies
inflated with gas

*

think about yourself
then think about purple clouds
it is poison gas

*

unaware of thorns
you make your way on the crown
termite visits Christ

what a shame to drown
as much so, looking away
Pacific Ocean

*

fat people swearing
broken seashells cut their feet
the waves won't relent

*

good night to this life
another won't resurface
from gloom's turbid sea

in this "V" of dirt
so many of life's premiers
dirt all around you

*

as you sit in dirt
starved beyond wondering why
what else can one say?

*

let me drink alone
at my bar or in the woods
weeping in true calm

for the love of God
please say something that's not dumb
before i kill you

*

yes, no, perhaps, yes
no, maybe, yes, no, perhaps,
yes, no, maybe, no

*

take off all your clothes
or else you will be alone
wait, that did not work

surrounded by cunts
every dream has been fulfilled
more and more and more!

*

cactus reminds me
Lilianna, i'm sorry
you are not a toy

*

everything is dumb
trapped by inability
to make something true

i have tried all night
and don't know what to write next
my wrist is throbbing

*

push and pull me back
crushed by your rounded saint's arms
i love you dream fawn

*

your ears grew stuck out
if you spread your arms as well
an orthodox cross

cock like a beer can
legs spread, floating on your back
overwhelmed by musk

*

hello brown spider
there is a lump on my wrist
i want to bite it

*

you are getting fat
from gin, from eggs, from candy
dampen vanity

this porch is fertile
hundreds of poems spreed here
it is stained with beer

*

your friends last night
a wine stain on the table
you all talk too loud

*

beneath painted eaves
starry night of spiders' eggs
cricket's lighted sky

terminal cancer
has never peaked my interest
like golf or football

*

the Virgin Mary
burned a cigarette in you
no, it was a mole

*

thirteen in a heart
with a finger down your throat
nothing good happened

my heart's dashed in tears
to know you are so tender
singing "Bleeding Love"

*

gag on a peanut
as you choke, run up a hill
so moles don't see you

*

acid coats my throat
exhausting my will to sing
i try every cure

he only smells leaves
whenever he sneaks past us
such bursts out the door

*

aren't you tired of this
inexhaustibly cut sludge
go feel something sweet

*

wash your fucking hair
Death can smell it from beyond
gross gross gross gross gross

i smelled your panties
you were in the other room
then we ate dinner

*

a cut on my nose
the door fell off its hinges
sinking foundation

*

hello evil death
if my body could be worms
i would crawl away!

Hark! a great potoo
worms, leeches and grubs listen
they want your best song

*

who is that outside?
is that my horror show dad?
actual zombie?

*

sending the message
"come over and hit on me…"
nothing's happening

sex has been ruined
by rank, childish demands
i don't care at all

*

taping every song
on KXLU FM
when it would come in

*

Michael as a child
it hurts to think of your life
say "hi" to Jesus

close to Mexico
memory of our desert
burning teenagers

*

burn up your campaign
that turns queers into dead sluts
Jesus dreams of it

*

cactus collection
i missed you so much i wept
this true hearts desert

grinding halt of sex
occurs when you are a jerk
so nothing has changed

*

Mariko Kaga
was so hot in her twenties
it must have been hard

*

are you friends for life?
why did it take twenty years
to say go away?

anything for you
hard relentless minotaur
until i can't walk

*

oh God is it you
whose voice i hear in my mind?
hope against crazy

*

unrevered by fate
though ultrarevered in hate
but write me back please

when we do break up
make sure to look in my eyes
remind me of you

*

unaware of both
arrogance and self-hatred
they walk arm in arm

*

every song you write
terrified in garbage heaps
no one ever hears

a fist through the wall
choking rust of pale boredom
like heavy metal

*

furious acne
fists in this shallow glamor
blue eyes eclipse Mars

*

bored by RnB
it's worse when you sing along
it used to be cute

writing to strangers
closer friends than you are now
God, i feel alone

＊

old gays are so cute
holding hands in pastel shorts
Similac laced dongs

＊

over Kaieteur Falls
my video camera
fell into Death's mist

dip earrings in wine
when your heart is broken up
suck suck suck suck them

*

an internal mist
should permit me to forget
the damage you caused

*

old man at my gym
working to stave off his death
lost in a daydream

wheel chairs are so hot
oh my God, Oh OH MY GOD!
roll on my hardness

＊

you fucking suck ass
that is why your bands are shit
and you flunk so hard

＊

burn a pile of books
finally we are moving
to forget this place

jasmine, calvin, nurse
roberta, doris, spunky
cats i've known and loved

*

i see you regret
neck crooked, minding over me
oh! my heart is light

*

in low light at bars
everyone says you look young
hold this feeling close

bigger intestines
bigger teeth, mouth, head, ears, drool
out shat by a dog

*

two young Southern men
close cropped heads banging against
witless histories

*

your teeth will fall out
vultures surrounding the hole
spit out unchewed meat

pull out the buck knife
scrape "why do they reject me?"
but just in the sand

*

insane dramatics
reduce what was love to brine
mixed with turds and sand

*

mosquito larva
flip around my small penis
both are disgusting

fuck! just let me read
a compromise in selfhood
making what was love

*

i love my brother
pray his broken life will heal
weeping on the plane

*

sit and make nothin'
Southern life weights down the plane
catalogs flipping

which is more evil?
to eat infant vagina
or infant penis?

*

in soap on the jeep
written "R.I.P. Grandma"
Cleveland, Ohio

*

list my grievances
silently in my dumb thoughts
over and again

i could pat your back
the way you used to pat mine
tears have filled my eyes

*

the thought seldom leaves
i want to become a girl
turn over bookshelves

*

someone will kiss you
when the time is the most wrong
it will never end

imperious thoughts
all over my life's work and love
it flaunts your lameness

*

the room is too hot
a mosquito bit your face
also, the show sucked

*

your birthday card says:
"grow up and do not come home"
you will have been warned

slave in a brothel
remembering your father
soaking with coal dust

*

if they were silent
the snow geese would disappear
a lake, frozen white

*

"Father-What-A-Waste"
was what we called the hot priests
what did they call us?

the air is freezing
is it too early for this
august in terror

*

to have been so free
then confused and in terror
wild pink bulls disbloomed

*

move from Korea
your playmates are Mexican
they just moved as well

it's cold in my house
come sleep with me fuzzy cats
i depend on you

*

gray air backs black trees
it will not be dawn for hours
everyone feels it

*

insane jealousy
of your popular success
i am a loser

psychopath babbler
what compels your endless speech
impose and impose

*

a genie has called
with a vulgar wish to grant
turn us into joy!

*

afraid of neighbors
thinking they cannot see cats
he flattens himself

listening to you
O Death, what chords free your touch
Muse! do not hide them!

*

criticize life's joys
gauzed by jealous loneliness
please please please like me

*

wish for perfect death
a hyena contact call
the last living sound

burn the field of corn
shoved down by the stench of ash
a crow collapses

*

Calvin makes a chirp
despite his width, his voice hides
what he wants to say

*

a voice like green tar
Judgement, my only lover
spews up in the South

Mary cries glitter
on the breast of queer lovers
she is so happy

*

with an ass like that
i bite it like an apple
and hear you cry out

*

the sun has gone down
she wants to eat an apple
i can't find any

a father and son
raping daughter and sister
molding at my mom

*

in 2 years, 2 floods
for what trial has He spared us
10 years of 10 floods?

*

your wife is a jerk
leave that lame illiterate
and kidnap your son

if you two want to
i'm easily persuaded
debased thus debase
*
autistic doctor
your father is Egyptian
cousin, my cousin

*
your ex-wife tacked you
on her lapel as a slave
exploiting genius

as popular youth
a horse will run into fire
transfixed by beauty

*

for most of this year
i don't know what i'm doing
rancidly un-new

*

right wing muthafucks
more frightened of love than goats
goring your mistress

snorting crushed green glass
exhaling a cloud of blood
invincible goat

*

let's make sweet sweet love
with armor, sword and a horse
gooing chivalry

*

opening my thighs
too late in the afternoon
blood drips from my ass

no one refuses
when i bite them on the ass
insatiable CHOMP!

*

a seashell is burned
blood soaks into the pink sand
crabs eat anything

*

you trim her white fur
animal crazed carousal
unaware as pets

the gnome lies face down
there is blood in his white hair
gnats eat at the wound

*

Calvin bites my hand
then demanding to be fed
sheds fur on my blouse

*

you want to have sex
but i did not eat enough
so i go to sleep

talking on the phone
while you fuck me in the car
say hi to your dad

*

little boy can't sleep
frightened of gigantic poop
he is 3 years old

*

darling Chola's glance
"time machine change my life's route!"
cried often enough

in field trip hotel
rolled up my pants to kick you
6th grade Brandon B.

*

Svetlana eat well!
the world hangs in the balance
anorexia

*

hang from the nostril
of cute, passed-out one-night stand
a buzzed and black fly

a single blue pill
dead center in your death bed
your ghost pleas with us

*

its just you and me
in this overdone hotel
one moth, one person

*

I can't stop sneezing
caterpillar like nostrils
that never pupate

incest makes us twins
it is fucking the whole world
that will save us both

*

wearing blue panties
you told me you were eighteen
swimming in belief

*

shouting "come to bed!"
i feel nauseous and flailed
stop yelling at me

killable infants
trample yellowed daffodils
on to nothingness

*

i pant and grovel
you could kill me with your thighs
ride your bicycle

*

no one talks to me
because i don't talk to them
the dream is over

awake and stabbing
the night that pumps your concern
requires nothing

*

last night i did dream
Gary Numan and Vince Clarke
were always married

*

i feel as a fool
whenever you talk to me
fucking manager

there was so much wealth
there was so little context
for all of your sins

*

eating a page of
bird songs from around the world?
oh, my fucking cat

*

sing out in your car
middle aged and thus alone
embraced by your voice

little Southern towne
wherein we are 4 years trapped
insignificant

      *

self-flagellation
over a long list of sins
the cat recites them

      *

Georgetown, Guyana
Fantastic Four airbrushed car
unbelievable

wanting to finish
impossible task master
thank you for the work

*

single prop engine
sitting next to the pilot
straight into a cloud

*

you have a bunny
so i love your self-hatred
thank you Laura H.

brutal trains assault
Durham's crumbled self-image
lie down on the tracks

*

i lie on my back
and looking up at the clouds
want to kill someone

*

so why do you care
if i hate this loathsome towne?
shadows your thin love?

finger cymbal chime
along with Bosnian hills
i have to pee bad

*

blown and cowering
in cloying Portland cottage
useless long fingers

*

poison berry vine
loops around a struggling calf
it gives up and waits

stand still and fuck off
blow gun you with poison darts
the tension unwinds

*

rubbing your nipples
while you sit and take a pee
wish for someone else

*

you waited two months
for her to flirt on your wife
she's not so special

a drunken letter
to your adorable friend
found its way to you

*

one one one one one
two two two two two two two
three three three three three

*

before we moved here
i had crushes on your friends
the new ones are gross

redeeming yourself
hard fought examination
save your family

*

when you try so hard
to make those people like you
the wren flies away

*

what should music be?
a titmouse hit the window
that is the answer

you wrecked their music
with you fouling red moustache
we all know you're dumb

*

a mirror descends
out the window of my room
glitter mats the lot

*

10 years of touring
my attempt is pathetic
swelling with old sweat

shame and death to you
puking on a chance for peace
jizz as a mortar

*

45 years old
tattooed, queer and muscular
steam room's censured glance

*

the dark red lipstick
that you asked me to buy you
redeems everything

i depend on him
as my brother gets older
to keep his mouth shut

*

i tried to like you
butterfly turns to larvae
10 years of trying

*

holding a baby
blighted by luxuriance
old friends turn sour

watermelon boy
with eyes crying its own seeds
perfectly shaped tears

*

are they just lonely?
fleas are filling up my house
i can't be your friends

*

lonely and working
study to save your mother
be at peace my sweet

finally over
betting on what i knew sucked
so long jive assholes!!!!

*

suck down insipid
cough rinds of unfunniness
fade through each date night

*

with two cats and scotch
waiting for you to come home
a flawless feeling

154

you spent the night like
disoriented sexy
sad to have fired you

*

go to church and wait
your LA childhood submerged
would you pray for it?

*

trying to be bad
little boys scream from a car
"Hey Cat! You Are Fat!"

press uncertainty
upon determination
thinking in circles

*

our crackpottedness
lends to knowing how to love
fuck it like a smurf

*

4, 5, oh haikus
"onsetsu" is syllable
the number won't fit!

Lightning Source UK Ltd.
Milton Keynes UK
UKOW051610310112

186389UK00001B/4/P